KIDS'

- HOW TO ORGANISE

by DA

A pocket-sized guide to organising and running parties for young people of all ages

All rights reserved. No part of this publication may be reproduced or transmitted in any form or by any means, electronic or mechanical, including photocopying, recording, or any information storage and retrieval system, without the written permission of the publisher.

© Printforce Limited, 1997

British Library Cataloguing in Publication Data
A CIP catalogue record for this book is available from the British Library
ISBN 0 948834 072

Illustrated by Phil Driver

Printed in Great Britain by
Shimwell Print Services Ltd. (01373) 832580

CONTENTS

INTRODUCTION 3

SECTION 1

PLANNING A PARTY 4
Reasons for having a party 5
Venue/date/time 6
Helpers 9
Numbers 10
Invitations 12
Decorations 14
Games 14
Prizes 16
Music/sound 17
Entertainers 18
Food & drink 20
Emergency programme 25
Themes 25

SECTION 2

PARTY GAMES 27
Coming-in games 29
Ice-breaking games 33
Circle games 36
Relay games 42
Team games 50
Quiet games 54
Pencil & paper games 60
Miscellaneous 63
Appendix 72

INTRODUCTION

We've all attended children's parties – either when we were children, with our own children or as leaders of youth groups. Some were no doubt excellent events, whereas others were possibly less enjoyable.

This book gives guidance and inspiration to anyone called upon to plan, organise and run a party for young people aged six to about 12 (parties become unusual beasts after that age and need several books and lots of courage!). It contains plenty of hints for avoiding often-made mistakes, such as having one child winning all the games, miscalculating on the amount of food needed and booking an entertainer whose act lasts an hour and whose material is more suited to adults visiting a nightclub!

The book is divided into sections concerning the planning, running and completion of parties, with a vast collection of games at the back of the book. The games are suitable for all ages, although some may be more popular with certain ages – children's moods change and what appeals one minute, may not be popular the next! We don't include any game which is complete rubbish – all have been tried and tested by my Cubs (the 7th Windsor (Old Windsor 'Baden' Pack), family and friends over many years and have been enjoyed by many! All games last approximately 10-15 minutes unless specified otherwise.

Enjoy the book, adapt the ideas for your own uses and, above all, remember that if you enjoy the party half as much as the kids do, then they'll enjoy it twice as much as you!

Dave Wood

Dedicated to Harry Harding-Wyatt, who enjoyed many of the games in this book.

PLANNING A PARTY

So, you've decided to run a party for a bunch of kids. Your friends will think you are mad but you know better – you have taken the time to read this book and are prepared to put up with any problems that might come your way in order that a group of young people can enjoy a fabulous, memorable party. If you prepare well, you and your helpers will enjoy the party and this will rub off on the children. If you perceive it as being a time-consuming, hassle-ridden nightmare, it could easily become one, so look on the bright side and you're halfway there!

There's a fair deal to think about when planning a kids' party, although if you've done it a few times before, you'll know that there is a basic formula for success and, once you've got that sorted, there is really very little else to do. The list of things to think about that we've printed here may look long but many tasks can be shared out among those you've roped in to help you:

- **reasons for having a party**
- **venue/date/time**
- **helpers**
- **numbers**
- **invitations**
- **decorations**
- **games**
- **prizes**
- **music/sound**
- **entertainers**
- **food & drink**
- **emergency programme**
- **themes**

Let's look at these elements one by one:

REASONS FOR HAVING A PARTY

Lewis Carroll wrote somewhere that *'If you don't know where you are going, any road will take you there'*. He could have been writing about kids parties because, if you don't work out exactly <u>why</u> you are running a party in the first place, it doesn't really matter what you do or how much you plan: the event itself will lack focus, direction and could well end up a confused mini-riot!

The party could be for:
- Christmas
- Someone's birthday
- A club/group anniversary
- Completing a long-term group project
- Tying in with a group activity, saint's day etc
- Marking the New Year, New Millennium etc

Confirming what the party is for will have a bearing on who is invited, where it is held, what the invitations and decorations will be like... and so on.

Kids' Parties

VENUE/DATE/TIME

Parties for large groups of young people aged six and over are best run in halls, rather than the homes of Leaders or parents, unless they happen to live in a Scout Headquarters or a sports centre! Kids need space to run around at the best of times and, given a party atmosphere and the inevitable excess of adrenaline, someone's home may not provide sufficient freedom to move around safely. (Note: people who run parties for Cub Packs in their own house are usually deemed to be doing it merely so they can claim on their home contents insurance in order to get someone else to pay for their overdue redecoration!)

Church and village halls, Scout and Guide Headquarters, Salvation Army halls and so on are usually the best bet and can generally be hired out for morning, afternoon or evening sessions for only a few pounds. School halls and council-run buildings, whilst seeming child-proof and accessible, are often very expensive, since there are caretakers who have to be paid, in addition to the running costs of the premises.

If you are a Guide or Scout Leader, then you will probably not have a problem finding a venue as your own Headquarters will probably do (although this shouldn't stop you looking at other possibilities just for a change or if you need more space).

Ensure that the venue is entirely suitable for your plans:
- Is it big enough for the numbers you are anticipating?
- Are there sufficient toilet facilities in good order?
- Is there a kitchen with food heating/washing-up facilities?
- Can parents deliver their children by car without too much difficulty?
- Are there any restrictions regarding noise?
- Is the location safe and unlikely to attract gatecrashers?

- Is there a telephone in case of emergency?
- Are there enough 13 amp sockets for your needs?
- Can you get access to the hall for setting up and clearing away or will you be charged considerably more for this?
- Do you need to remove your refuse after the event?
- Are there any restrictions regarding putting up decorations (with sticky tape, plastic 'tak', pins etc)?
- Are there brooms available for when it comes to clearing up?
- Are the keys readily accessible?

Once you have located the venue and confirmed its availability, work out the date and time for your party with those who will be helping you. It is best to hold parties on Saturday or Sunday afternoons (although you might choose to avoid the latter if it's a school day on the Monday as your party might wear the kids out!). As for the length of the party, think about what you will be doing and how much the young people will be able to cope with.

As a general rule, parties should last around two hours. Much shorter and you will find that you won't have time to fit in the 'traditional' requirements (games, tea etc.) whilst if they are much longer, kids and adults alike will get tired, restless and possibly bored and fractious.

Printed overleaf is a very basic outline programme to show you how the time rushes away:

Kids' Parties

(2.00pm	*setting up)*
3.00pm	Coming-in game/activity
3.15pm	Game
3.30pm	Game
3.45pm	Game
4.00pm	Tea
4.30pm	Activity/entertainment
4.50pm	Game/Father Christmas
5.00pm	Depart
(6.00pm	*Clearing-up completed)*

We'll talk about the detailed elements of the programme later on in this book. It is important to plan a programme (not just have a heap of ideas and play it by ear) and ensure that the helpers all have copies of it. You should also have a spare game or two in reserve in case other elements run short.

You will have noticed that we are running our party from 3.00-5.00pm. Experience shows that this is possibly the best time for afternoon parties as it encompasses teatime and enables parents to go shopping or watch the soccer whilst their children enjoy the party! If you start at 2.00pm or earlier, guests may only just have had lunch and too much running around may not be a good idea, especially if you are in charge of the mop and bucket. Start later and the young people may start to flag as the evening draws on – remember that the clearing-up will take around an hour and you might not wish to wipe out your evening, having already spent your afternoon on the event. If you are planning an outdoor party with an elaborate tea or barbeque, plus a treasure hunt or wide game, three hours may be needed.

If you are running your party in place of your regular weekly youth group meeting, the above may not apply to you. Most meetings last an hour and a half so it might be worth considering stretching this by 15 minutes either end, to let you fit everything in and make all the effort worthwhile. You may find, however, that you will need to set up the hall the night before (after any other hall users have gone) or, if the hall is in use during the day, immediately prior to the party.

As above, allow an hour for setting up, although this can be reduced to 30 minutes if you plan it well. Have the equipment (including prizes) for each game/activity in separate boxes; have the decorations in a bag and allocate two helpers to devote their time to decorating the room; have the sound/music equipment tested and ready to install – again, allocate a helper solely to this task; have any pre-bought food in a box ready to hand to the person allocated the job of looking after the food.

HELPERS

Whilst youth leaders may, on occasions, be used to running weekly meetings with a ratio of one adult to ten or 15 young people, parties are different. Whether your party is for 14 or 40 children, six helpers (in addition to the 'leader' of the event) are often sufficient to cover most eventualities:

- Two to run the current game/activity
- Two to prepare the next game/activity
- Two to be sorting out the food

Even though you may be used to running games single-handedly, running a party game on your own, with lots of excited youngsters while the other adults are hidden away preparing food, can be a bit scary – besides, there's safety in numbers!

If you can press-gang parents to help, ensure that they are given tasks, however small, or they will inevitably congregate by the food table and chat, while a hard-pressed leader struggles to run a game that isn't going very well! A typical useful (if not glamourous) job is to wander around with a black plastic sack scooping up discarded wrapping paper, food, streamers and so on.

NUMBERS

There's not much that can be said about how many people to invite, other than remembering to keep within the capacity of the building you are using and that you have sufficient help to supervise them all. If there are likely to be less than 12 people attending, a vast hall may give an 'empty' atmosphere. Avoid this by simply making the hall smaller by draping groundsheets or blankets over ropes strung across the hall. This will give a more cosy feel to the party.

Avoid too wide an age group at your party. Games run with young people of widely differing abilities usually end up a bit lop-sided and younger children will feel left out. Obviously there may be the odd older or younger sibling who has to come along so their parents can help, but don't feel that they must join in with every game and activity.

Older children like to feel important and can help prepare food or blow up balloons, while much younger children could potter around playing with their favourite toys and watching the games.

To show you how children vary in their expectations and capabilities at parties, here's a rough guide to what the age groups are like:

SIX year-olds like to help prepare by colouring in invitations and will have short attention spans and seemingly endless energy when it comes to games, so have lots of active games and plenty of space.

SEVEN year-olds will understand the rules of games better than younger children and can therefore play fewer, but more 'complicated', ones. Leadership abilities start to emerge at this age and team games can be used more.

EIGHT year-olds seem to overwhelmingly prefer single-sex parties (younger than eight can usually be mixed, depending on the children involved). Lively, competitive games and lots of food and prizes are required here.

NINE year-olds are very competitive and like to 'show off'. Any game in which individuals can display their skills are popular, especially team games, as long as those in charge of the game ensure that all competition is healthy and not disruptive.

TEN year-olds will usually do whatever is asked of them at a party and will join in everything with enthusiasm. Have a good mixture of games and activities and you won't go wrong!

ELEVEN year-olds and older start to feel awkward at traditional parties, especially if both sexes attend. It is often better to organise outings of smaller numbers (4-10 children) or hold outdoor theme parties, indoor themed discos (both of which can be mixed sex and fancy dress).

If it is a birthday party you are organising, remember that the birthday boy/girl will have looked forward to the event for a long time and will have high expectations of it. Even though they will be excited, it is important that they remember to meet and greet the guests and say 'thank you' for any presents that come. Siblings often feel left out, so it is a good idea to give them special jobs to do, such as looking after coats, helping with the food and so on.

INVITATIONS

Work out who you are inviting and create invitations, making sure they include ALL of the information needed:

- **Where is it?** *(should you include a map?)*
- **When is it?** *(date and time for start and finish)*
- **What is it?** *(what is the party for?)*
- **How much?** *(should they bring food/drink with them?)*
- **What else?** *(fancy dress? Special instructions?)*
- *RSVP?* *(to whom should they reply, and by when?)*

Post or hand deliver the invitations to ensure that everyone invited gets one – and so that their parents are aware of the party. Avoid handing them out on meeting nights as they may not make it home and guests may miss out on the event.

The invitations need not be too complicated. You can buy blank invitations from High Street stationers, on which you fill in the details. If you are running a theme party, you could create invitations using a word processor or typewriter and decorate them accordingly, sending guests photocopies. Alternatively, simply photocopy and distribute the Printforce 'Instant Invitation' printed opposite, filling in the blanks and erasing details you don't need with correcting fluid:

You are invited to a

PARTY

to be held at _____

on _____

from _____ *to* _____

RSVP to:
_____
_____

please bring
some party food
with you

PLANNING

Kids' Parties

DECORATIONS

The type of decorations you decide to put up will depend on the type of party you are running:

- **Christmas:** *paper decorations, tinsel, Christmas tree, fairy lights, balloons*
- **Birthday:** *banners, balloons, streamers, bunting*
- **Themes:** *depends on the theme!*

You need not spend much money on decorating a room or hall. Ask around and collect up people's old unwanted decorations or ask local shopkeepers if they have any old decorations they use in their shops that you could have. If this book enthuses you sufficiently and you think that you will be running lots of parties in the future, why not look around the post-Christmas sales, where you can always find decorations for half price or less.

GAMES

No party is complete without a selection of games. These are usually fairly competitive, although a leader armed with a bag of mini-chocolate bars or similar prizes can ensure that all those taking part get a prize, whilst the winning player or team could get something ever-so-slightly more substantial. If the game is run well and is good fun, winning seems to fade into insignificance and the quality of the prizes ignored.

The bulk of this book is taken up with an array of games and activities to delight all ages. Choose your games carefully and think through how you are going to run them before you start.

When preparing your list of games, write down anything that comes into your mind and add a note of roughly how long they take – the games in this book all take approximately ten-15 minutes to explain and run.

Then, put the games into order – whilst it might seem easier to run two or three relay games in succession, to save time and effort organising teams, it is best to alternate between the various types of game. This ensures that players always feel involved and that something different is always happening (one relay game is, after all, very much like another!).

Try to maintain a mix of noisy and quiet games and those which involve everybody at once or individuals.

Here are some do's and don'ts for running party games:

> **DO**............make sure you know the rules.
> **DO**............have all the equipment ready.
> **DO**............have your programme at hand.
> **DO**............ensure someone is getting the next item ready.
> **DON'T** ....let a game continue if it goes wrong. Stop, explain the rules and start again.
> **DON'T** ....let games run over time if at all possible, however well it is going.
> **DON'T** ....have more than one game per party in which players are 'out' as they can get bored and restless.

One last suggestion. If you have a group of rowdy youngsters, or a particularly large group (20 or more), you will find that many party games either take too long or become difficult to control. An excellent idea is to organise a series of 'games bases' which small teams visit in turn. This way, you will fit in more games, all players will be involved and the whole event will be much easier to control.

You will need one adult to be in charge of each base. Each adult will run a game which lasts five minutes or so thus, with four bases, you will need to allow 20 minutes plus five minutes or so on top to allow for changeovers. The best games to use are those found in the 'Quiet Games' section of this book. Teams should be of no less than four and no more than eight in number and should move around the bases in a clockwise direction – adults must hold onto their groups until all are ready to move on (at the signal of the leader-in-charge).

PRIZES

Hopefully, the games will be fun enough to play that prizes are not necessary. Guests will, however, expect to each win something during the party so, as we mentioned earlier, mini chocolate bars can be dispensed to each member of winning teams so that individuals receive at least one prize.

'Swag Bags', 'Going-home Bags' or whatever you like to call them are useful for house parties and birthday parties in halls but are NOT needed for Christmas parties or parties run by youth groups. Traditionally, these were introduced in order that it was not just the person whose birthday it was who ended up with all the presents.

Paper or plastic bags with each guest's names on can be pinned up along a length of string, and they are encouraged to put into their bag any prizes they win during the party. Near the end of the party, a leader could check the bags and pop extra goodies into them to ensure that everyone goes home with something – even if it is just a piece of cake and a balloon!

There are several companies who can supply very inexpensive 'goodies' to use as prizes or put in swag bags – a few are noted in the appendix at the back of this book.

If you are running a fancy dress contest, or guests come in fancy dress to fit in with a theme, remember to have a small prize for the best costume as a reward for the effort they (and their parents) have made. Don't make a big thing of the judging or of the prize since, by rewarding one child you are disappointing everyone else – move swiftly onto a game and all will be forgotten.

MUSIC/SOUND

If you are a youth leader and are used to leading games and activities in a hall, don't automatically assume that your voice alone can be heard by a bunch of noisy, excited partygoers! If you can get hold of a simple public address system (which could simply be a domestic karaoke machine with microphone) to help your voice be heard you will find that the guests respond quicker – and your voice lasts longer.

Music is an essential party ingredient, whether it is just used for games such as 'pass the parcel' or 'musical bumps', or as a background for other games, for eating or even dancing to. Do not rely on a domestic cassette player – whilst you only turn them up to a quarter of their volume at home and assume that full power is deafening, put it in a Scout hall with lots of noisy kids and it simply will not be heard.

Either borrow a purpose-built karaoke machine (many families own these nowadays) or find someone with a loud, heavy-duty cassette player. You could try moving your stereo hi-fi system from your home into the hall as this should be quite loud – but check your insurance first! Either way, test the machine in the hall a few days before the event to ensure it is suitable.

The music you play is up to you and depends on the party and the people involved. If you only want music for games like 'pass the parcel' you will need a piece of lively music, with catchy words and tunes that guests can sing along to if they want. Also, they need to be quite long with no sudden gaps or pauses in the middle of the song – how many times have you been caught out playing 'pass the parcel' by the record suddenly ending just as you restarted the game?

The group 'Jive Bunny' produces a range of albums that are perfect for these purposes as they are continuous, lively and contain well-known songs – check your friends' record collections and High Street stores now!

ENTERTAINERS

It is not usual for youth groups to include a children's entertainer in a party programme but they are popular for parties involving children aged from about four to ten years. It is always best to book an entertainer following word-of-mouth recommendation as you will have a fair idea of what they are like.

Ensure that you book the entertainer well in advance, and that you confirm the details in writing. The person will need to know the exact venue (provide a map if in an obscure Scout Headquarters); the time he should be performing; how long the show will be; how old the audience will be and how many of them there will be; how much space he will have – and the payment details. In 1997, the average cost of a half-hour show by a popular entertainer during the day was about £50, although this varies depending on time of day and how much in demand the entertainer is!

If you do not know of any entertainers, check out the classified adverts in your local newspaper or in the various telephone directories under 'Children's Entertainers'. Many will lend you a video of them in action to help you decide who to book.

Under this heading comes good old Father Christmas. Santa likes to visit children's parties but, if he's too busy, he has been known to send along one of his helpers, dressed in much the same way. Younger partygoers will greatly appreciate the appearance of Santa at the end of a party, especially if he comes bearing a sackful of gifts (which need only be sweets or cheap toys wrapped in Christmas paper).

His arrival could be heralded by everyone sitting down in a circle and singing a Christmas song or two – he is known to be especially fond of 'Jingle Bells' and often appears during this song, if it is sung loudly enough! He can then move around the circle distributing gifts – adults are needed to ensure everyone stays seated and does not mob the poor old chap. It may be an idea to welcome him in and sit him on a chair, asking the guests to visit him in turn.

It is important that, if it is one of Santa's helpers that will be attending, nobody sees him getting changed as it will spoil the effect. He should stay in character throughout and disappear afterwards with a cheery wave, leaving partygoers to open their gifts.

Children of eight-plus may have a slightly cynical view to a visit such as this. When my Cub Scouts (aged 8-11) muttered that they didn't believe in Santa I simply suggested that if they didn't believe in him, he obviously couldn't come and that he would give his presents to someone else. I then got them to chant out loudly *'I Believe in Father Christmas!"* at the tops of their voices and, lo and behold, Santa appeared and gave them all presents!

FOOD & DRINK

I like sausages. Any party you decide to invite me along to should therefore include copious supplies of cocktail sausages please. Many other people like them, too, so they make an easy-to-prepare item for your tea table – whether or not I'm on the guest list!

If you are holding a party for a son or daughter's birthday, you will have to organise the catering. The benefit here is that you can decide exactly what will be eaten, the diet can be balanced (well, as balanced as party food can get) and it will probably be eaten around a table.

Hall-based parties for youth groups are different, usually because they are for larger numbers and because there is no one to pick up a potentially big food bill! It is usual, in these cases, for guests to be asked to bring some party food along with them to add to the tea table. If you do not ask individuals to bring specific items, you may not get a good cross-section of sweet and savouries, although in all my years of running parties like this I've not had a problem. Besides, the kids don't care! It may be an idea, in the invitation, to ask them to bring some food and to list a range of things to help prompt them. Don't just say 'Crisps and sausage rolls' because that maybe all you end up with! I emphasised 'sausages' on my last invitation and eight boys brought bowls of sausages in addition to other bits and pieces. Yum!

It is, however, up to you to provide drinks. Cola, lemonade and orange squash are really all you need. Use plastic disposable cups, but only fill them half full as they are easy to knock over when full. If you like spending money for no real reason, buy paper/plastic cups from stationers that are decorated with Christmas or birthday scenes. If you realise that money is better spent on prizes etc., buy cheap plastic ones from discount shops for a tenth of the price and smile smugly to yourself at how switched on you are. Younger children might like to decorate cheap cups the week before the party, by sticking on pictures cut from old wrapping paper offcuts.

You might also like to have a supply of chocolate biscuits and bags of crisps in reserve, just in case the guests' provisions run out.

Handy hint: Fed up with broken crisps on the floor, caused by bad stacking of food on plates? Forget those family-sized bags which tip into a bowl (which you probably forgot to bring anyway) – buy cheap 25g bags of crisps from discount supermarkets so that each guest can have a packet. This will be sufficient for them and will mean that the crumbs stay in the packets!

Here's a list of items you might like to ask guests to bring:

- sausages(!)
- crisps etc
- sandwiches
- chocolate biscuits
- cakes
- sausage rolls
- fruit
- samosas
- savoury snack biscuits
- Twiglets™
- dips
- sticks of carrot, cucumber etc
- raisins
- cheese

Remember to have lots of large plates and bowls – few halls have these available so you may need to bring your own.

Unless guests will be sitting around a table in a formal 'tea time' environment (which can take ten minutes extra than 'grazing' methods), guests can visit a buffet and return with their pickings to sit in groups of their choice on the floor. Adults should ensure that guests are not greedy – popular items (chocolate biscuits, for example) could be put out a few at a time to help prevent this and to ensure that everyone gets a good choice.

Space precludes me from including too many suggestions for party food – hunt through recipe books for ideas or keep an eye open in case Printforce publishes a party food recipe book in the future!

To give you a few starters, though, here are three simple ideas for party fayre:

• **ORANGE BOATS:** A simple but eye-catching and popular food is one created by my sister for her children's parties. Whether the theme was pirates, fairies, explorers or magicians, everyone looked forward to the 'orange boats'. These are made by cutting oranges in half (one orange per four guests), scooping out the insides and filling the halves with orange jelly. When the jelly sets, carefully cut the halves in half (or into three) to give what looks like segments of an orange. Put these on a plate and stick a cocktail stick through the jelly to act as a mast, add a paper sail and you've got a tasty orange armada!

• **CHOCOLATE PASTRIES:** Roll some pastry out so that it is quite thin, scrape off any loose flour and spread some chocolate spread onto the top side of the pastry. Fold it in half and cut it into slices about 1-2 cm wide. Put in the oven on a greased baking tray, near the top, for ten-15 minutes or until the pastry is golden brown. Remove from the oven, place on a wire rack and sprinkle icing sugar.

- **MINI KEBABS:** This takes the old cheese and pineapple sticks a bit further. Prepare small chunks of cheese, pineapple, mushroom, grapes, raisins, ham etc and push them at random onto cocktail sticks or small kebab sticks. These can be arranged on a plate – saving you having to prepare a foil-covered potato!

The liberal use of natural food colourings can quickly turn everyday food into themed food: sandwiches can be painted with markings using watered-down colourings; sausage rolls can be made with coloured pastry and drinks can take on a different appearance completely!

Cutting items such as sausages and sandwiches in strips can turn them into items of food relevant to the theme and you might be brave enough to cook hot food for a special theme. The best party I remember from my childhood was a cowboy themed one in my back garden, run for my sister and I by my parents – the food consisted of a 'chuck wagon dinner' (sausages, beans and bread) which filled everyone up and was enjoyed by all. On reflection, it was probably far easier to organise than even the simplest traditional party food selection.

Finally, please remember that not everybody's diet (medically controlled or otherwise) is the same as yours. Ensure there are meat-free alternatives to sausage rolls (vegetable samosas and spring rolls are popular) and, most importantly, avoid having peanuts. Smaller children can easily choke on peanuts and an increasing number of people are developing peanut allergies, where just traces of peanuts can be fatal if eaten. Ensure that you are aware of your guests allergies and requirements when preparing the party and, if a child has a nut allergy, request that no food brought along contains any nuts whatsoever, in case the allergic child eats it by mistake.

Avoid everyone rushing to the food table at once. There are three simple games I use (one per party) which enable the flow of visitors to the buffet to be controlled, whilst giving those waiting their turn a bit of fun:

• **POOR PUSSY:** Players find a space and sit down. The Leader crawls on all fours to players at random and pretend to be a cat, saying *"Meeow,"*. The player pats the Leader on the head, saying *"Poor pussy."*. If the player does this without smiling or laughing, another leader lets him or her up to visit the food table, if they smile or laugh, they remain seated until it is their turn again. The Leader moves to another player at random and continues until all have been to the food table.

• **MEMORY POCKETS:** Players sit randomly in front of an adult who sits on a chair. He has clothing on with several pockets: trousers, waistcoat, jacket. In each pocket he has an object and shows the players what is in each pocket. He then asks a player at random to identify what is in a particular pocket. If she guesses correctly, she can visit the food table, if not, she waits to have another turn later. When those remaining seem to know where each item is, swap the objects around so the players can see and start again.

• **UNHAPPY PARTYGOERS:** Players sit a random on the floor and an adult goes to them in turn and, without any physical contact, tries to make them laugh or smile. Players may not close their eyes nor cover their mouths. If a player remains glum, he may visit the food table. If he smiles or laughs he must wait for another go.

EMERGENCY PROGRAMME

If you have an entertainer booked who doesn't turn up (she breaks a leg, gets lost or just forgets), someone forgets the equipment for a planned game or everything runs more smoothly and quickly than planned, you may need an emergency programme.

All you really need is this book and 30 seconds to hunt down the games that don't need any equipment, or a piece of paper with the names of two or three spare games (and the necessary equipment).

Better still, buy the Printforce book *'Panic Ideas'*, available from where you bought this or from the address on the back cover, which contains scores of easy-to-run games and diversions to cover up those little emergencies.

THEMES

Leaving Christmas parties aside for a moment, there are often times when you feel that it would be a good idea to run a party on a particular theme. It may be for a birthday or special anniversary or simply to try out the games in this book! Whatever the reason, if you decide to have a theme, it is best to 'go the whole hog' or don't bother with a theme at all.

Everything from the invitations, decorations, prizes, games and food can (and should) be linked into the theme, which could be:

- Space/science fiction
- pirates
- explorers

- cowboys
- cartoon characters
- cops and robbers
- circus
- Hallowe'en*
- the 1950's
- Medieval
- beach party *(even in winter!)*

(Many people are uneasy with the religious aspects of Hallowe'en, so please take great care when planning such a party so that nobody is offended)

Ensure that it is very clear on the invitations that there is a theme and that (if you want them to), everyone should attend in fancy dress. If you are asking the kids to dress up, it is only right for the adults to as well – a bunch of ten year-olds dressed as clowns can feel out of place amongst the adults dressed in Scout or Guide Leaders' uniform, for instance!

It might seem daunting to turn every game and the food into the theme but it is possible with only slight modifications. Look at any game in this book and I'm sure you can easily turn it into a themed one but substituting the word 'players' with 'clowns' or whatever, and making whatever they do fit in with the theme simply by renaming the equipment used. (I remember changing a game using a yellow plastic duck and a football into one suitable for an Australian-themed beach party by simply calling it 'Emu and the Egg'!

It is, however, slightly harder to theme the food, especially if guests are bringing and sharing the bulk of it. You can always provide a few themed food items yourself, depending on the theme.

PARTY GAMES

What makes a party game different to any other game that youth groups play? Usually it is simply the inclusion of food or sweets and prizes! Take a look in any games book, especially those published by Printforce, and you will find a range or popular games that can be used to great effect in a party environment, just by adding a prize element and some sweets! What follows, however, is a carefully selected collection of tried-and-tested party games designed specifically for parties.

Before you start reading the following games, please study the following points to help you and the players get the most out of the games:
- Give the game a name, even if it's a brand new one you've made up – players can ask for it again if they enjoy it.
- Vary the games you choose to suit the occasion (noisy, quiet etc).
- Have enough players to play it properly.
- Explain the rules slowly, logically, simply and clearly.
- Be sure that players know the playing area boundaries.
- If you need equal numbers in teams, make the last person in the short teams go twice - don't make extra players drop out.
- Have all the equipment you need ready before you start.
- Don't explain the rules until all players are in the starting position.
- Even if it's a well-known game, remind players of the rules so that everyone plays it the same way.
- If a game doesn't work well to start with, change the rules if you think it will make it work better.
- Make sure that every player is capable of playing the game or they will feel left out and unhappy.

Kids' Parties

- When pairing players to play against each other, try to pick pairs of equal size, weight and/or age.
- When the game is being played, be enthusiastic and encourage players, this will brush off on them..
- Don't let a game last more than 10 minutes, however popular it is.

PICKING TEAMS

- Number players off at random one, two, one, two... and so on. Ones play twos.
- Players stand in a line, with the tallest at one end, shortest at the other. They are numbered off alternately (one, two, one, two...). Ones play twos.

NOTE: 'Numbering Off' means that you give players in a team, or in a circle, a number each, starting from 'one'.

COMING-IN GAMES

It is useful to have a game arranged that needs little explanation and just needs one adult to supervise, to enable other adults to welcome children, speak with parents, accept food for the tea table and prepare the first game.

Smelly Boxes

Equipment: 20 empty 355mm film canisters, plus a paper and pen per person.

Preparation: fill each canister with a different smelly item, such as pickle, toothpaste, pepper etc. Drill a 5mm hole in each lid and stick them on with glue or tape. Number them and place them on tables around the room.

• When guests arrive, hand them a sheet of paper and a pencil. They wander around the room and, by smelling inside the canisters, write down what they think is inside.

• Award a prize later on when you have collected and judged the answers.

Spot the Celeb

Equipment: paper and pencil per person, sheets (see below).

Preparation: cut out 20 or so pictures of famous people and glue them to separate sheets of paper.

• Stick the sheets around the hall.

• When guests arrive, hand them a sheet of paper and a pencil. They wander around the room and look at the pictures, writing down the name of the person (real or fictional).

• Award a prize later on when you have collected and judged the answers.

Feely Bags

Equipment: *about 15-20 feely bags (see below), paper and pencil per person.*
Preparation: *put 15-20 items into separate plastic or cloth bags, seal them and suspend them around the room.*

• When guests arrive, hand them a sheet of paper and a pencil. They wander around the room and, by feeling the objects through the bags, write down what they think is inside.

• Award a prize later on when you have collected and judged the answers.

What's on Television?

Equipment: *sheets (see below), pens and paper.*
Preparation: *Cut out 20 (illustrated) programme details from television magazines, cutting out the title of the programme but leaving the details and cast list. Stick them onto individual sheets of paper and number them.*

• Stick the paper around the hall and ask the players to identify the programmes and write them on a sheet of paper which you have already written the numbers 1-20 down the side..

Adverts

Equipment: *Adverts (see below), pencil & paper per player.*
Preparation: *Cut out approximately 20 advertisements from newspapers and magazines and affix them to sheets of paper, giving each one a number. Remove all references to the product by cutting out trademarks and names.*

• Pin the adverts up around the hall and, when the players arrive, hand them a pencil and a sheet of paper (preferably pre-numbered down the side from 1-20).

• Players wander round the hall and try to identify what the product is the adverts are about.

Who am I?

Equipment: *sticky labels (see below).*
Preparation: *prepare dozens of sticky labels, each of which carries the name of a well-known real or fictional character or person, or of a job (such as a dustman, cook etc). There may be duplicates.*

• As they arrive, players have a sticker put on their back and try to identify the name on it by going to someone who reads the sticker and MIMES what is written. When a player guesses it, he tells the Leader what it was and swaps the old sticker for a new one and carries on.

Where is This?

Equipment: *photographs (see below), photocopy of street map and pencil per player.*
Preparation: *Take photographs of local landmarks, such as well-known buildings, libraries, station, road signs etc. Affix these to sheets of paper and give each picture a number.*

• Pin the pictures up around the hall and, when the players arrive, hand them a pencil and a photocopy of a map (use map which may be copied according to the copyright law).

• Players wander round the hall and try to identify where on the map the items in the photographs are and mark them with the relevant number on their map.

Autograph Hunting

Equipment: *pens and prepared lists*
Preparation: *produce copies of a list of 'qualities', such as: Someone who is left-handed, Someone with a brother. Someone with glasses, Someone with black hair, Someone with a tooth missing etc.*

- Players try to find others with those qualities and ask them to sign their names in the space on the paper.
- Players may only sign for ONE quality on a player's sheet.

Sealed Orders

Equipment: *'sealed orders' (see below).*
Preparation: *write lots of tasks pieces of paper and fold them up.*
- Upon arrival, players are each given a 'sealed order' which they must try to do as quickly as possible.
- Tasks can include: 'Get the signature of someone whose second name contains the letter N'; 'Find out the names of someone's pet dog'; 'Find Peter McHugh and introduce him to Timothy Wood'; etc.
- When a task has been carried out, players report back to the leader to get a new sealed order.

Matched Halves

Equipment: *card (see below).*
Preparation: *write the names of cities and towns onto separate pieces of card and cut them in half. Hide the cards with the first parts of the words on around the hall.*
- Players arrive and are each given a card with the second half of a word and must locate the card to complete the word.
- When players complete their word they return to the leader, tells her the name of the city/town and swaps the card for a new one.

ICE-BREAKING GAMES

The following games can be used as 'first games' or in place of 'coming-in games'. They are good for helping children to get to know one another which should help the rest of the party go with a swing!

Circle Circuit

Equipment: a football.
- Players stand in a large circle and throw the ball to each other at random across the circle (but not to their immediate neighbour).
- If a player catches the ball he says his name and throws the ball on to someone else.
- After four or five minutes of this, stop the game and explain that from now on, players say the name of the person they are throwing the ball to (whilst it is in the air).
- A few minutes later, stop the game and explain that, from now on, players throw the ball to someone and says (for example) "Throw it to Emma". The player who catches the ball throws it to Emma and calls out the name of someone for Emma to throw the ball on to.

Human knotting

Equipment: none.
- About six to 12 players stand in a tight circle holding their arms out in front of them (have two or more groups if necessary).
- They hold hands with two DIFFERENT players (not their immediate neighbours), one in each hand.
- The group must then try to untie the knot and end up in one large circle with their hands still linked, ideally facing inwards.

Kids' Parties

Expert Interview

Equipment: none

- A Leader becomes a television interviewer and welcomes the 'audience'. He invites one player to sit with him at the front and this player is introduced as 'the world's greatest living expert on...' whatever you want! It could be an expert on gardening, electronics, aircraft navigation systems, making sweets... or whatever.
- The interviewer asks questions, to each of which the 'Expert' must provide as intelligent an answer as possible.
- After a few questions, choose a new 'expert'.

Hello hello hello!

Equipment: none

- Players wander around the hall and, when they make eye contact with someone, they introduce themselves.
- After four minutes, players sit in a circle and each must try to name everyone in the circle (in turn).

Circle Names

Equipment: none

- Players have a sticker with their names written on it stuck on their chest.
- The Leader begins a rhythm by slapping his thighs, clapping and then clicking first his right then his left fingers, giving a '1,2,3,4' rhythm.
- The Leader says his name on the FIRST finger click, and another player's name on the SECOND click. That player must then, on the next first click, look at someone else, say her own name and that other person's.
- After five minutes or so, remove the stickers and continue to see if players can remember everybody's names.

Skin the snake

Equipment: None.
- Players form up in teams of five or more and stand up one behind the other, close together and with their legs apart.
- Player One in each team bends down and puts her RIGHT hand through her own legs, from front to back, grabbing hold of Player Two's LEFT hand.
- Player two does the same, taking Player Three's left hand with his right hand.
- The Leader says 'Go!' as soon as all the teams are ready and, on this signal, the last player in each line crawls through the legs of his team, still holding hands with his neighbour. The player standing in front of him follows him through the legs, remembering not to let go.
- The first team to stand in a line, holding hands wins.

Dizzy David

Equipment: none
- Players sit in a circle and someone starts by saying their first name after a description which begins with the same letter as their name(eg: Dizzy David, Playful Peter, Joyful James, Wild William, Jokey Janet etc...
- Players continue in clockwise direction around the circle – players lose a 'life' if they get stuck.

CIRCLE GAMES

Shooing Horses

Equipment: *two chairs (each with four legs), two blindfolds, seven plastic cups or shoes.*

- Players sit in a large circle with the two chairs placed some distance part in the centre.
- Two players are chosen at random and each sit on a chair while they are blindfolded. The seven cups are scattered around the playing area (within the circle).
- The two players must then crawl around and try to locate cups ('horseshoes') and, one at a time, return to their chairs ('horses') and put a shoe on.
- First player with four shoes on their horse, and with them sitting on the horse, wins.
- Players may 'borrow' from other horses, but not if the horse is being sat on at the time!

Shooting Rabbits

Equipment: *a stick (or similar)*

- Players ('rabbits') stand in a circle around the leader (the 'farmer'), who has the stick (or 'shotgun').
- When the farmer points the shotgun at a rabbit and says "Bang!", the rabbit 'dies' and sits on the floor UNLESS he put his hands up either side of his head and wiggled them about, like rabbits' ears (these miraculously deflect the pellets!).
- Moreover, the two plays on either side of the rabbit being shot will also die unless they put their ear up on the side next to the shot rabbit.
- Any player doing the wrong actions, or reacting slowly, is out and sits down. Players must be alert as to who their new neighbours are.

Pass the Parcel Strikes Back

Equipment: *A prize, a newspaper; brown paper, wrapping paper, sticky tape, a cassette recorder, paper strips with 'forfeits' written on them, wrapped sweets.*

• Prepare the usual parcel, although in between each layer of paper attach a strip of paper bearing a 'forfeit' to a wrapped sweet.
• Players sit in a circle, the music starts, and the parcel is passed around until the music stops.
• Whoever has the parcel removes one layer of paper and, if they find a forfeit, must follow the instructions. Forfeits could include: 'Be the fairy on a Christmas tree', 'Be a chicken laying an oversized egg,' 'Lie down and drink a glass of water'... etc.

Knee Tapping

Equipment: *a (thin, light) rolled-up newspaper and a chair.*
• Players sit in a wide circle with legs crossed (or on chairs).
• One player becomes 'Wally of the Week' and stands in the middle, with the rolled-up newspaper.
• 'Wally' wanders round the circle and taps a player at random on the knee, puts the paper on the chair and sits down in the space previously occupied by the person she tapped. That person, as soon as he is tapped, gets up, grabs the paper once it is on the chair and tries to swipe Wally on his back before he sits down.
• If Wally gets to sit down without getting swiped, the other player becomes 'Wally of the week' and the game continues. If Wally is swiped, he has another turn as Wally.
• If the paper is dropped by Wally, he must return and put it on the chair – this obviously gives whoever was hit more of a chance to grab it and swipe him!

Going to Market

Equipment: none.

• Players sit in a circle and the leader starts by saying "I'm going to market and I want to buy an Apple" (or anything else starting with 'A').
• The next person around the circle repeats the sentence, including the apple, and adds something beginning with a 'B'.
• This continues around the circle – can everyone remember the ever-increasing list?

Circle Seat

Equipment: none.

• Players stand in a tight circle, facing inwards. On the signal, they all turn to the right, so that they are facing anticlockwise round the circle.
• On the second signal, they slowly lower themselves so that they are sitting on the knees of the player behind.
• If done in two or more teams, the first to have everyone sitting down like this wins!

Robber, Where Are You?

Equipment: Two blindfolds, a short rope (or scarf).

• Players sit in a big circle and a player becomes a 'robber'. His ankles are tied together.
• Two others are blindfolded and are the 'cops'.
• The cops stand in the circle while the robber moves about freely.
• The two cops try to catch the robber by listening for him.
• The cops can say *'Robber, where are you?'* as often as they like, to which the robber must always respond by clapping his hands twice.
• When the robber has been caught, select new cops and robbers.

Balloon Catching

Equipment: *a few balloons.*
• Players sit in a circle and are numbered off. An extra player (with no number) stands in the centre of the circle with two inflated balloons.
• He throws the balloons in the air and calls out two numbers (you did remember to tell him what the numbers go up to, didn't you?). The two players with those numbers leap up and try to grab a balloon before it reaches the ground.
• Whichever player gets to their balloon first stays in the middles and throws the balloons for round two.

All Those...

Equipment: *One chair per player.*
• Chairs are arranged in a circle, with one player sitting on each chair.
• Two or three players stand in the middle and secretly decide on something that will be common to a number of those in the circle and one of them calls this out. For example: *'Everyone wearing a blue sweatshirt.,'*. All those wearing blue sweatshirts should then change places with each other.
• The three in the middle also try to get a seat. The next three left standing have to think of something else.

Kids' Parties

The Old School Bus

Equipment: None.
• Players sit in a circle and are divided into groups which are given the name of something in 'the old School bus', such as 'the wheels', 'the windows', 'the kids', 'the teacher', 'the sandwiches'... etc.
• The Leader tells a story about a school trip and, whenever he says one of the above items, the children with that name stand up quickly, turn around and sit down again.
• When the Leader says 'The Old School Bus', everyone stands up, turns around and sits down.
• Nobody wins, but then nobody loses either!

Heads and Hands

Equipment: A football.
• Players stand in a large circle with the Leader in the centre.
• The Leader passes a ball to players at random. As the ball leaves her hands she says either *'Heads'* or *'Hands'*.
• Whoever the ball was passed to must perform the opposite action to what the Leader says. (ie: if the Leader says *'Heads'*, the players catch it; if she says *'Hands'*, players head it back.

Spin the Plate

Equipment: A plastic or metal plate or tray.
• Players sit facing inwards in a circle and are numbered off.
• A player stands in the middle, spins the plate on its edge (on the floor) and calls out a number.
• The player with that number tries to catch the plate before it stops spinning. If she fails, the player in the middle repeats the process, if she succeeds she swaps places with the person in the middle.

Eye Eye!

Equipment: none
- Half the players sit in a large circle, facing inwards. The others each stand behind a sitting player.
- Choose a sitting player to be 'It'. After a short pause, she has to wink at another sitting player.
- When someone has been winked at he leaps into the middle of the circle before the player standing behind him has a chance to place her hands on his shoulders.
- If the player gets to the middle without getting stopped, the sitting team wins a point, if not, the standing team wins.
- Choose someone else to be 'It' (perhaps he who was winked at) and the game continues.

Emu and the egg

Equipment: a football, a plastic duck (or similar)
- Players stand around a leader in a large circle.
- The players pass the duck (or 'emu') clockwise around the circle. Meanwhile, the leader throws the football (or 'egg') to players at random, who catch it and return it.
- Anyone dropping the emu or the egg is out and sits down where they are. Players throw the emu to their new neighbours, over the heads of anyone who is out.

RELAY GAMES

Traditionally the most popular sort of party games, these will encourage healthy competition and lots of cheerful noise. Try to select teams of roughly equal ability and numbers. If teams are of equal numbers, the winning team is usually the first one whose members have all completed the task (and whose members are sitting quietly in a straight line). With teams of unequal numbers, either set a time limit and see how many players per team had a turn or get a player in understaffed teams to run twice. A small prize (sweets) for each player in a winning team soon ensures that everybody wins something during the party.

Nudgers

Equipment: one ping pong ball (or similar) per team.
• Players sit in relay form and, on the starting signal, Player One in each team bends over and nudges their ball to the far end of the hall, picks it up and runs back to set off Player Two, and so on.
• Try it with a tangerine!

Scarecrow Dressing

Equipment: per team: a big coat, large pair of wellies, hat, scarf, large gloves, huge trousers.
• Players sit in relay form with one in each team chosen to be the 'scarecrow' and who stands at the far end, arms outstretched, and with the clothes at their feet.
• On the starting signal, Player One in each team runs up and puts ONE item of clothing on their scarecrow, before returning to set off Player Two.
• First team to dress their scarecrow wins.

Bag Bursting

Equipment: at least one small paper bag per player.
• Players sit in relay form with their supply of bags at the far end of the hall.
• On the starting signal, Player One in each team runs up, grabs a bag, inflates it and bursts it in their hands before running back to set off Player Two.

Newspaper

Equipment: several sheets of newspaper.
• Players sit in relay form and, on the starting signal, Player One in each team picks up two sheets of paper and uses them like stepping stones to get to the far end of the hall, whereupon she picks up the paper and runs back to set off Player Two.
• First team to finish wins.

Peanut and Fork

Equipment: a monkey nut and a fork per team.
• Players sit in relay form and, on the starting signal, Player One in each team picks up the fork, balances the monkey nut (unshelled peanuts) on it and runs to the far end of the hall and back to set off Player Two.
• If the nut is dropped the player must stop, pick it up, re-balance it and continue.

Flap the Balloon

Equipment: some balloons and magazines.
• Players sit in relay form and, on the starting signal, Player One in each team picks up their magazine and tries to flap their inflated balloon to the far end of the hall.
• They pick up the balloon and return to set off Player Two.

Chin Pass

Equipment: a tennis ball or orange per team.

• Players stand in relay form. Player One holds an orange under her chin and passes it to Player Two who collects the orange under his chin without the use of anyone's hands.

• First team to complete a 'there-and-back' circuit wins.

Spoon Threading

Equipment: teaspoons, string.
Preparation: for each team, prepare a 10m length of thin parcel string, on the end of which a teaspoon is tied securely.

• Players stand in relay form with Player One holding the spoon and string.

• He threads the spoon through his sleeve, down his jumper and hands it to Player Two, who does likewise.

• This continues until the team is joined together – first team to complete wins.

• Some groups might like to try the advanced level where the spoon is threaded down trousers/skirts as well!

Apple Bobbing

Equipment: apples, one bowl of water per team.
Preparation: Cut the apples up into pip- and skin-free chunks (this is more hygienic than using whole apples, whose skin sometimes causes cut gums).

• Players sit in relay form with a bowl of water, containing apple chunks, at the far end of the hall in front of them.

• On the starting signal, Player One in each team runs to their bowl and tries to grab a chunk of apple using only their teeth, not their hands.

• When they have a chunk, they return to their team to set off Player Two.

Flap the kipper

Equipment: per team – a fish shape cut from paper or card, a magazines or newspaper.

- Teams sit in relay form and a 'kipper' and magazine is placed at the front.
- On the starting signal, Player One in each team flaps behind the kipper until the air wafts it to the finishing line some 5m away. They pick up the kipper, run back to their team and set off Player Two.
- First team to complete wins.

Dressing Up Relay

Equipment: per team: a big coat, large pair of wellies, hat, scarf, large gloves.

- Players sit in relay form with their pile of clothes in front of them at the far end of the hall.
- On the starting signal, Player One in each team runs to the clothes, puts them on and runs back to their team, where they must take the items off.
- Player Two then puts them on, runs to the far end and takes them off, running back to tag Player Three, and so on.

Party Polo

Equipment: Polo™ mints, thin drinking straws (or similar).

- Players stand in relay form and each hold a straw in their mouths.
- Player One has a Polo™ mint on their straw which they pass to Player Two, and so on. No hands are allowed. If a mint is dropped it can be retrieved but must be given back to the player passing the mint, not the one receiving it.
- First team to complete a 'there-and-back' circuit wins the prizes.

Kids' Parties

Yogi Bobbing

Equipment: for each team – some boiled sweets, some Maltesers™ a bowl of water and a plate of flour (go easy on the flour – a handful is sufficient).

Preparation: Bury ten sweets in each plate of flour and drop ten Maltesers™ into each bowl of water (these float and don't get too soggy!).

• Teams sit in relay form with, a short distance away, their bowl of water and then, beyond that, the plate of flour.
• On the starting signal, Player One in each team runs up, tries to grab a Malteser™ with their teeth (no hands allowed) and quickly run to the plate to grab a sweet in the same fashion. Having done so, the players (whose faces now resemble Yogi Bear!) return to set off Player Two.
• Have a towel at hand!

Biscuit Bobbing

Equipment: ring biscuits with holes in the centre, string.
Preparation: Rig up a 'washing line' and, from it, suspend one biscuit per player.

• Teams sit in relay form and, on the starting signal, Player One in each team runs to the line and, without using her hands, grabs a biscuit in her mouth and eats it off the string, returning to set off Player Two... and so on.
• A messier version can be run using ring doughnuts!

Mad Hatters

Equipment: Four hats, elastic, safety pins.
Preparation: Join the hats together in two pairs with a 50cm length of elastic and a couple of safety pins, so that they may be worn, but with difficulty.

- Players form into two teams, within which they pair off and sit side by side, next to the other team (to form four lines in total), with the joined hats in front of the team.
- On the starting signal, the first pair in each team stands up, puts on the hats and runs to the far end of the hall and back again. If a hat falls off, they must stop and pick it up.
- They then

Pea Soup

Equipment: Dried peas; a cup and saucer per team; one drinking straw per player.

- Teams sit in relay form with a cup and saucer in front of each team at the far end of the hall. The saucer contains 12 dried peas and the cup is empty. Each player has their own straw.
- On the starting signal, Player One in each team runs to the far end and sucks one pea from the saucer, drops it into the cup and runs to the back of his team for Player Two to repeat the process.
- If a pea falls on the floor the player must pick it up, put it in the cup and start again.
- First team to move all peas into the cup wins.

Skiing Race

Equipment: Two shoe boxes, two garden canes and four saucers per team.

- position the saucers upside down in a line in front of each team to act as slalom posts.
- Players sit in relay form with the two boxes and canes in front of them.
- On the starting signal, Player One puts a foot in each box and, with a cane in each hand, slides like a skiier to the far end of the room and back, swerving around the slalom posts.
- Player Two repeats the process and so on.

Pea in a Bottle

Equipment: drinking straws, dried peas, a milk bottle and a saucer per team.

• Players sit in relay form with several peas on a saucer in front of them. The milk bottle is in front of their team at the far end of the hall.
• On the starting signal, Player One in each team uses his straw and sucks a pea onto the end. He then runs to the bottle with the pea still attached to the end of the straw and drops it into the bottle. He returns to set off Player Two.
• After five minutes, who has the most peas in their bottle?

Film Case Towers

Equipment: Seven empty 35mm film canisters per team

• Players sit in relay form with seven film canisters in a pile in front of each team.
• On the starting signal, Player One in each team runs up and puts one canister on top of another, the second (when tagged) runs up and builds up the tower, adding one canister before returning set off Player Three.
• If a tower falls down, the player may rebuild it. Whose tower is tallest after, say, four minutes?

Balloon Coaxing

Equipment: A 1m length of string and a balloon per team.

• Players sit in relay form. A balloon and piece of string is placed in front of each team.
• On the starting signal, Player One in each team holds the ends of the string in either hand and 'drags' the balloon up the hall, touches the far wall and back to his team to pass the string to Player Two, who repeats the process.

Izzy Dizzy?

Equipment: none
- Players sit in relay form.
- On the starting signal, Player One in each team runs to the end of the hall, puts a hand on the ground and goes round in a tight circle five times, keeping his hand on the floor.
- They then return to their teams to set off Player Two.

Matchbox Noses

Equipment: a matchbox sleeve per person.
- Players sine up in relay form and Player One pushes a matchbox sleeve onto his nose.
- On the starting signal, he passes the sleeve, without using his hands, to Player Two's nose, who then passes it to Player Three and so on.
- First team to complete wins.

Birthday Cake Bake

Equipment: None.
- Players sit in relay form. Each Player One is given the name of an ingredient needed to make a cake, such as Eggs. Player Two is flour... and so on.
- A Leader describes the making of a birthday cake. When an ingredient is mentioned, the player with that ingredient hops to the end of the room and back, so that the leader can continue.
- If the leader says 'Birthday Cake', all players hop to the end and back!

Kids' Parties

TEAM GAMES

Team games are different from relay games in that they are usually for two teams and do not necessarily require them to be sitting down. They often mean that everyone is involved in the game at the same time.

Mummy Game

Equipment: plenty of cheap toilet rolls.

- Players select a member of their team to be the 'mummy' (in the Egyptian sense of the word).
- On the starting signal, teams take the toilet rolls (two per team should do) and start to wrap their mummy in paper.
- After six minutes of this, judge the best looking mummy and award prizes.
- Then, on a signal, get the mummies to all burst out of their wrappings! You could also, by the way, give a small prize to the team that puts its litter in the bin the quickest!

Tail Tally

Equipment: a 1m strip of material per player.

- Players form into four teams, one player in each becomes a 'catcher'. The other players each have a strip of material tucked into the waistband of their trousers or skirts to form a 'tail'.
- On the starting signal, catchers try to grab as many tails as they can in four minutes.
- Anyone losing their tail rests at the side of the hall and can not play unless the catcher from their team gives them a captured tail.
- Award prizes to the team whose catcher has captured the most tails.

General Post

Equipment: *paper and pen.*
Preparation: *write the names of four local locations or major cities, one per paper, and pin these up in the four corners of the room.*

- Players sit in teams, one team in each corner of the room.
- The leader announces that he wishes to send a letter from London (for example) to Edinburgh, whereupon the teams in the London and Edinburgh corners stand up change places, walking, not running.
- The last person to be sitting down in the corner loses a point, from a starting total of ten, for their team.
- Players use different methods to change places, depending on what the leaders say:

> **Letters** = *they walk*
> **Telegram** = *they run*
> **E-mail** = *they run and do one head-over-heels*
> **Postcard** = *they hop*
> **Parcel** = *they crawl on hands and knees*

Ten Passes

Equipment: *a football.*

- Players divide into two teams and a ball is thrown into play.
- Whoever catches the ball passes it to someone in his team who passes it to someone else. Players try to throw the ball ten times among the teams.
- Players must not pass the ball back to the one who passed it to them and no physical contact is allowed. Player can block and intercept the ball.
- Start the counting again if the ball touches the ground or if an opposing player intercepts it.

Welly Boot Game

Equipment: *Three giant-sized wellington boots.*
- Players sit in two teams down either side of the hall and are numbered off. they remove their shoes.
- The three boots are placed on the floor in the middle of the teams.
- The leader calls out a number and the two players with that number run to the middle and try to put on two boots. The first player to do so wins.

Balloons-Up

Equipment: *ten balloons per team, a whistle.*
- A Leader throws the ten balloons into the air (one after another).
- One team tries to burst all the balloons within two minutes.
- At the same time, players from the other teams try to stop the balloons being burst by hitting them into the air.

Note: Ensure that players do not push each other, or use anything sharp to burst the balloons.
- Repeat with a different team trying to burst the balloons.

Tunnel Goals

Equipment: *a football.*
- Players divide into two teams and line up 3m apart, facing each other and stand, legs apart, with their feet touching those of their neighbours in their team.
- A Leader throws a football between the lines and each team tries to score a goal by throwing the ball through the legs of the other team's players.
- Players may defend with their hands and must not move their feet. Use a second ball to liven things up a bit.

Volleyball-oon

Equipment: *length of rope, balloons.*
Preparation: *suspend the rope across the room about 1.5m from the ground.*

- Players divide into two teams and stand on either side of the rope, as in volleyball.
- A balloon is thrown into play and players try to make the balloon touch the ground on their opponent's side. The balloon must go over the rope.

QUIET GAMES

Here's a selection of games suitable for immediately after teatime, or to use as 'games bases' (see page 25).

Rolling Stones

Equipment: ten small stones (or similar) per player.
- Players sit in a tight circle, hiding their stones in their laps.
- A player takes some stones, holds them in her closed fist and asks the person on her left "How many stones in my hand?"
- The player has to guess how many stones the first one is holding. If he is right he can keep the stones. If wrong, he gives the first player TWO stones as a penalty.
- Player two repeats the process and asks player three... and so on around the circle.
- Who has the most stones at the end of the game?.

Pig

Equipment: a pack of playing cards
Preparation: Sort out the cards so that there are four cards of a kind per player (all the fives, sixes etc).
- Players sit in a circle and have four cards dealt to them each at random, face down.
- The Leader says 'Go!', and everyone looks at their cards and, at the SAME TIME as everyone else, passes ONE card face down to their LEFT. This should be done quickly – players chant *'One, two, three, PASS'* to keep the momentum up.
- When a player has four matching cards she puts a finger on her nose. Others watch for anyone doing this and, if they see someone doing it, must do the same. The last one to put their finger on their nose loses that round.

We Don't Like Fish Pie

Equipment: none.

- Players sit in a circle with a Leader who asks the player on his left 'Do you like fish pie?' he must reply, 'No, I like...' and mentions something to eat or drink which does NOT contain the letter 'F'.
- The leader asks the same question of player Two, and so on around the circle. Anyone who gets stuck moves and sits on the right-hand side of the leader and the circle shuffles round to accommodate him.
- A different food can be chosen and the game continues from where it left off.

Tommy Smartie

Equipment: A saucer, lots of coloured chocolate beans.

- Players sit in a small circle with the saucer in the middle. On this are placed ten chocolate beans.
- One player leaves the room while the others choose a chocolate bean to be 'Tommy Smartie'.
- The player comes back and picks up the sweets one-by-one.
- When they pick up the chosen one, everyone shouts 'Tommy Smartie!' and the player must stop.
- More sweets are added and the game continues with a new player.

Make me a Star

Equipment: newspaper.

- Players are challenged to tear a five-pointed start from a sheet of newspaper.
- Award prizes for the best attempts.

Matchmakers

Equipment: bottle, six matchsticks per player.
- Players sit in a small circle with the bottle in the centre.
- Players take it in turn to place a match onto the bottle (or on top of any matches already there).
- If a player knocks any matches off, she must take and keep all those knocked off.
- The object is to be the first player to get rid of their matches.

Buzz

***Equipment:** none*
- Players sit in a circle and someone says 'One', the next says 'Two'... and so on round the circle.
- Any number with a **3** in it (13, 23, 30...), or which is divisible by **3** (6, 9, 12...), must be said as *'BUZZ'*.
- If someone forgets to say Buzz when they were meant to, a new player starts with 'One' and it continues as before.

Whisker Whipping

***Equipment:** A plastic face mask, tissue/toilet paper.*
***Preparation:** block up the eyes with tape (on both sides). Cut long, thin strips of paper and stick these on the mask's chin, to act as whiskers.*
- Players sit in a wide circle around one player who is wearing the mask.
- A leader chooses a player who must try to creep up and pull ONE whisker from the mask without being pointed at by the the player in the middle. Whiskers can be exchanged for small prizes.

Cream Crackered

Equipment: *plenty of cream crackers.*
• In small groups, players are timed, one-by-one, to see who can eat three dry cream cracker biscuits and then whistle!
• Have glasses of water available for when they finish!

Crossed Uncrossed

Equipment: *a pair of scissors*
• Players sit in a small circle and a Leader passes a pair of scissors to one of them, saying *"I pass these scissors to you crossed"* or *"I pass these scissors to you uncrossed."*
• The player takes the scissors and passes them on to someone else in the 'correct' way.
• It doesn't actually matter whether or not the scissors are crossed, but whether the person passing the scissors has his or her legs crossed! See how long it takes for everyone to work it out and learn the secret.

Mystery story

Equipment: *None.*
• Players sit in a small circle while one leaves the room. A Leader explains the game to the others.
• The player returns and is told that the others have invented a story. His job is to learn the story by asking questions which can have a 'Yes' or 'No' answer. He asks each player a question in turn around the group.
• There is, of course, no story! Players answer yes or no depending on what the LAST word the questioner asks is: If the last word they say ends in a CONSONANT, the answer must be YES, if the the last word they say ends in a VOWEL, the answer is NO.
• The Leader may have to suggest suitable questions if someone gets stuck, but an interesting story is bound to emerge!

Electric current

Equipment: none
- Players sit in a circle and hold their neighbours' hands behind their backs. Someone leaves the room and another player is chosen to be a 'generator'.
- The player returns, stands inside the circle and the generator starts an electric current by squeezing the hand of ONE of his neighbours. The current is passed on around the circle, until it gets back to the generator. It is then sent back the way it came.
- Some players are chosen to be of electric gadgets (toaster, TV, alarm clock etc) and make a noise when the current passes through them.
- The chosen player has to chances to guess who the generator is.
- Repeat with new players taking on the various roles.

Letter Changing

Equipment: none
- Players sit in a circle and a Leader says a three-lettered word.
- The player next to her must change a letter in that word to produce a different word.
- When a new word has been said, the next player changes a letter to make another new word.
- For example, a word such as DOG could become DIG, then DID, then BID, BAD, HAD, HAT, HIT... etc.

Paper Tearing

Equipment: newspaper.
- Players are challenged to tear a continuous strip of paper from a standard sheet of newspaper.
- Award prizes for the longest unbroken strips.

Pop Pip

Equipment: *none*
- The leader turns to a player and says "Pip". The player must say "Pop".
- If the leader says "Pop", the player says "Pip".
- Is the leader says "Pip pop pip", for example, the player says "Pop pip pop".
- How complicated can it get before the players get confused?

Job Centre

Equipment: *None.*
- Players sit in a circle and one leaves the room.
- While she is out, the others think up a job for her.
- When she returns, she has to ask each player in turn a question what she needs to buy to help her in her job. (If she was a Judge, the players would say a wig, hammer, robes... and so on.
- How long does it take her to work out what job she has been given?

Snowball Story

Equipment: *None.*
- Players sit in a small circle and a Leader begins to tell a story. At an exciting point he stops and he chooses someone to continues the tale.
- The Leader stops the storyteller after a short while and chooses someone else to carry on. How unusual a story will you get?

PENCIL AND PAPER GAMES

Squiggles

Equipment: *Pencil and paper per player.*
Preparation: *draw a selection of squiggles on separate sheets of paper and photocopy them.*

• Each Player is given a sheet and adds as many lines as he wishes to turn it into a picture. Give a prize for the best or funniest pictures.

• Players could also do a simple squiggle themselves and give the paper to someone else to convert into a picture.

Tim's Game

Equipment: *several large sheets of paper per person, pens.*

• Players each have a pen and a large sheet of paper and draws the shape of given objects as near to their exact size as possible, such as a bottle top, a pound coin, matchstick, playing car etc.

• Compare the drawings with the real objects and award plenty of prizes at random for good efforts.

Animal magic

Equipment: *A large sheet of paper per team, pens.*

• Players sit in two teams down one end of the hall and are numbered off.

• A Leader gives each player a part of an animal to draw, but the parts must not run in any logical order (e.g. player one draws eyes, player two toenails or claws...).

• On the starting signal, Player One in each team runs up and draws their part and returns to set off Player Two. Award a prize for the best picture.

Charades

Equipment: *paper (see below).*
Preparation: *write a number of well-known film, show, book and television titles onto individual pieces of paper.*

• Choose a player at random and give them a piece of paper. They must mime the title, using the traditional actions to determine whether it is a film, book or whatever, and how many works the title contains.
• Whoever guesses correctly has the next go at acting.
• This can be run in two teams.

Who am I?

Equipment: *paper (see below)*
Preparation: *A list of occupations that may be mimed, e.g. baker.*

• Players sit in teams in corners of the room.
• One player per team goes to the Leader who whispers an job to them.
• Players return to their teams and mime the job. If a player guesses the job being mimed, the next player goes to the leader to get a new job to mime.
• The first team to have mimed all jobs on the list is the winner.
• Adults may be needed to observe teams to ensure that those miming do not speak.

Party Quirks

Equipment: *paper (see below)*
Preparation: *prepare a list of strange 'quirks', such as 'he thinks he is a cow', 'he is a sports commentator', 'she thinks you are her mother'... and write each one onto separate pieces of paper.*

• Choose one player to be the party host, who stands in front of the others.

- Give a player a piece of paper and ask them to go to the 'party', acting out the 'quirk' written on the paper.
- The host must try to work out what the 'quirk' is.
- Send other guests with new quirks along as you wish.

Wordplay Jackpot

Equipment: *sheets (see below), pencils.*
Preparation: *prepare a copy of a grid for each player with a word written across the top and with the following written down the side: a bird, a town, a boy's name, a girl's name, an animal, a football team (or whatever).*

- Players (in pairs) have ten minutes or so to fill in the blanks on the grid.
- If the word along the top is 'TRAINS', for example, they would need to write down a bird beginning with 'T', one beginning with 'R', 'A'... and so on, then a town starting with each letter etc.
- When all have finished, go through each space and let them mark their own sheets. If anyone has the same word as them in a space, nobody scores a point. If they have a word that nobody else has, they score one point.
- The pair with the highest score wins.

	T	R	A	I	N	S
A BIRD						
A TOWN						
A BOY'S NAME						
A GIRL'S NAME						
AN ANIMAL						
SOCCER TEAM						
A COUNTRY						

MISCELLANEOUS

Clapping hot and cold

Equipment: none.

• Players sit on the floor (at random) and someone leaves the room.
• While he is gone, the others decide on an object in the room they want him to touch, or something simple they want him to do with an object (such as move a book from the floor and put it on a table).
• He returns and is told whether he must touch something or perform an action.
• The other players begin a slow handclap, getting louder and faster when he gets closer to the object, and slower and quieter when he moves away from it.
• He should soon work out what he has to do!
• Chang the player and choose another object.

Pin the Tail...

Equipment: a blindfold, a large picture and a suitable tail or nose (see below), a pen.
Preparation: Make a large picture of the face of a reindeer, clown (etc, as appropriate to your theme), or a side view of another animal (or simply buy a poster or sheet of wrapping paper with a single picture on it). Make a nose/tail and put a blob of BluTak™ or similar on the back.

• Players take it in turns to be blindfolded, disorientated and pointed towards the picture, where they stick the nose/tail on. Mark where the nose was put by putting the players initials on the picture and award a prize for whoever was closest.
• This is best for small groups.

Kids' Parties

Musical Hats

Equipment: *roughly one hat per player.*
Preparation: *write numbers either inside the hats or on stickers placed inside the hats (either cheap party hats or a collection of real ones).*

• Players are given hats, with the exception of about four or five players.
• When the music starts, players without hats try to grab a hat for themselves which they place on their heads. Nobody is allowed to hold onto a hat.
• When the music stops, a number is called out and the player with that numbered hat wins a prize (or does a forfeit!).

Grandma's Footsteps

Equipment: *none.*

• All players except one stand at one end of the hall. The other player ('grandma') stands at the other end with her back to the others.
• Players try to creep up to grandma and touch her shoulder.
• Grandma can, at a any time, turn around – anyone she sees moving is sent back to the start.
• The first to successfully touch grandma becomes the next grandma.

Jelly Feeding

Equipment: *bowls of jelly, wooden spoons, aprons (adapted bin liners will do), blindfolds.*

• Players sit facing each other across a table, in pairs.
• Both are blindfolded and each holds a wooden spoon.
• They must try to feed *each other* with jelly from the bowl on the table!
• Run this as a spectator game or in small groups.

Sitting Standing

Equipment: a chair.
- Players stand in front of the leader, who is sitting on a chair.
- If the leader stands up, the players sit down, and vice-versa.
- Try to confuse them by half sitting!
- The last player to respond is out and stands at the side of the room.
- Give this a twist by getting them to put their arms in the air when yours are by your side, and vice-versa, mixing the two actions as you wish.

Question-only Conversation

Equipment: none
- Two players stand in front of the others and try to hold a conversation with each other. They must only ask QUESTIONS, though *("How are you?" "Why do you ask?" "Aren't you ill?" "Hadn't you heard?" "Should I have done?" "Weren't you there when I told the others?"... etc).*
- Whoever is first to respond with a statement, rather than a question, sits down and another player takes her place and the conversation continues.

Instant Fairy Tale

Equipment: None.
- Guests are chosen at random to form a 'cast' who will perform a play in front of the others, who form the audience.
- A traditional fairy tale is chosen and a leader gives each of the chosen children a character to play.
- The group must try to act out the story from beginning to end without any discussion, planning or rehearsal.
- Repeat with other children and other stories.

Doughnut Challenge

Equipment: one doughnut per player.
• Players are given a doughnut, one at a time or in small groups, and must try to eat it without licking their lips!
• Anyone who manages this feat wins a prize.

Do the Locomotion

Equipment: one chair per player.
• Players sit in a very large circle on chairs with one person standing in the middle.
• That person begins to travel around the inside of the circle imitating a form of transport: aeroplane, pogo sticks, ice skates etc.
• Every now and then he taps seated players gently on the knee and they must follow on behind him, copying the mode of transport.
• After a short while, the first person calls out *'All Change!'*, at which point everyone tries to sit on a vacant chair.
• There will be one person left without a chair and they repeat the process with a different form of transport.

Earth, Air Water

Equipment: a football.
• Players stand in a circle around a leader, who holds a football.
• The ball is thrown to players at random and the leader calls out either 'Earth', 'Air' or 'water'.
• The player to whom the ball is passed must catch it and, before quickly throwing it back, call out the name of a type of animal, bird or fish (as appropriate).
• If they say something that someone else said previously, they are out and sit down.

Sticker Patrol

Equipment: coloured sticky labels.

- Six players are chosen to be 'attackers' and they each have four coloured stickers.
- A leader turns the lights out and the attackers must try to find the other players and stick labels on them.
- Players are allowed to take the labels off but, when the lights are turned back on, everyone 'freezes'.
- Leaders then see how many players have been tagged by the attackers – and then another six players can be attackers.

Musical Chairs Strikes Back

Equipment: half the number of chairs than there are players

- The chairs are put in a circle, facing outwards.
- Players form two teams, with one standing inside the circle, each player holding the back of a chair.
- The other players each sit on a chair.
- The music starts and the players on the outside get up and walk around the circle clockwise. When the music stops they run back and sit on the chair they were first sitting on.
- The last one to sit down is out but remains seated on his chair for the rest of the round.
- Award prizes for the last two left playing.
- Then swap the teams around.

Do This — Do That

Equipment: None.

- Players stand in a circle around a leader.
- The Leader says *'Do this'* does an action such as waving a hand or nodding her head. The players must copy her. If the Leader makes an action and says *'Do that'*, players should ignore her.
- Anyone who does the wrong actions loses a 'life'.

Musical Chairs

Equipment: music source, one chair per player.
• Chairs are lined up in two rows, back-to-back, there being one chair less than the number of players..
• Players troupe around the line of chairs when the music plays. When the music stops they try to sit on a chair.
• The player with no chair to sit on is out and another chair is removed.

Musical Statues

Equipment: music source.
• Players dance about to the music. When the music stops they stand perfectly still.
• Anyone moving is out. Repeat the process until you have a winner.

Musical Bumps

Equipment: music source.
• Players dance about to the music. When the music stops they suddenly sit down.
• The last person to sit down is out. Repeat the process until you have a winner.

Washday Blues

Equipment: a rope and newspaper per team, plus two clothes pegs per player.
• Players tear the shape of various clothes and peg them onto the washing line (one item per player).
• Prizes go to whoever makes the best clothing or the smartest entire washing line-full.

Jelly Darts

Equipment: *Packets of stale jelly which are well past their sell-by date, poster paper and pens.*
Preparation: *draw a target on the paper, which is pinned up on a wall.*

- Players are each given three cubes of stale jelly and take it in turn to throw them, one at a time, at the target.
- If the jelly is warm and damp it will be sticky and will stick to the target easily.
- Who can get the highest score?

Mousetrap

Equipment: *Whistle,*

- Two players hold their hands to make arches and stand at one end of the hall. Another pair does so at the other end.
- On the starting signal, players run around clockwise, passing under each arch.
- When a whistle is blown, the arches drop and probably catch a player. Caught players form pairs and make other arches in the circle for players to pass through.

Chocolate Dice

Equipment: A large bar of chocolate, pair of or oven gloves, hat, scarf, plate, knife, fork, very large dice.

- Players sit in a circle, with all the above the items in the middle. They take it in turn to throw the dice.
- Anyone throwing a 'SIX' runs to the middle, puts on the hat, scarf and gloves and tries to eat the chocolate, one square at a time, on the plate using the knife and fork.
- As soon as the six was thrown, the dice continues around the circle and anyone throwing a six takes his place.

Shopping Lists

Equipment: Five lists of items (see below), felt pen.
Preparation:
• Four adults stand on a chair each around the room. They each have a different list of items in their shop. Each shopkeeper has a problem: one has a sore throat, one is hard of hearing, one cannot see very well and one is a slow thinker.
• Another Leader asks players to find the shop selling 'blue potatoes' (for example).
• Players go to a shop and ask the shopkeepers if they stock the item. The shopkeepers over-emphasise their disabilities for a short while so that players get fed up and try another shop.
• The correct shopkeeper soon identifies himself and players must form an orderly queue in front of him. The last five players in the queue get a felt pen mark on the back of their hands as a penalty point.
• Give a prize to those with fewer than one penalty mark after seven items have been called.

Happy Families

Equipment: a pack of home-made happy family cards with five family members eg: Mr Gibbs, Mrs Gibbs, Master Gibbs, Miss Gibbs, Baby Gibbs.
• Players sit in a circle and are each given a card.
• On the starting signal, players pass the cards from one to another clockwise until the leader calls 'Stop!'.
• Players must then shout out the name of his family try to find the other members.
• When a family is complete they must sit together on a chair: father first, then mother, brother, sister and, last of all, baby.
• The first family to sit, complete, on a chair are the winners and get a prize each.

Balloon Football

Equipment: *lots of balloons.*
- Players pair up and sit in two lines, facing their partners with their legs outstretched so that their feet touch..
- Two other players are chosen as goalkeepers and stand behind each team. A Leader throws a balloon (or two, or three) into play and team try to get the balloon over the heads of the opposing team.
- A goal is scored if a balloon touches the ground on the opponent's side.
- The team with the most goals gets the prizes.

Fishy Tails

Equipment: *string, paper.*
Preparation: *Prepare 1m lengths of string, each of which has a cut-out fish shape attached to one end.*
- Players each have a 'tail' secured into their waistbands, so that the fish lies on the floor.
- On the starting signal, players charge around and try to stamp on other players' fish.
- If a player loses their fish they must wait at the side of the room.
- Award prizes for whoever is left at the end.

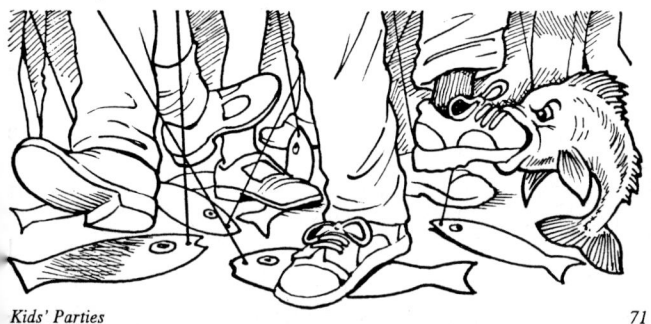

APPENDIX

(All details correct at time of going to press.)

Suppliers of Party Prizes/Games etc:

- **Baker Ross Ltd,** Unit 53, Milmead Industrial Estate, Mill Mead Road, London N17 9QU. Tel: 0181 808 6948

- **Party Party,** Euroway Business Park, Swindon SN5 8SN. Tel: 0990 243444

- **Peeks of Bournemouth Ltd,** Tuckton, Bournemouth, Dorset BH6 3BR. Tel: 01202 417777

Games/activity books from Printforce:

- **Panic Ideas**
- **Really Wet Games**
-
-
-
-
-
-

+ address?